Poetic Joy

Michael Lumsdaine

BookLeaf
Publishing

India | USA | UK

Presentation by *BookLeaf Publishing*

Web: www.bookleafpub.com

E-mail: info@bookleafpub.com

ISBN: 9789358313031

First edition 2023

To my Mom, Dad, Brother, Aunt, Nana, Grandma, Grandpas, and my Nana. In memory of my great grandma who lived to be over 100 years old.

ACKNOWLEDGEMENT

Thanks to Mrs. Nelson, for getting me involved in this challenge.

PREFACE

Poems of joy, and reflection, and everyday things, written daily by a middle schooler.

Wind

Twas a windy night
For all, no power in sight
Trees dance in the air

The Wonders Of Music

2

Oh, the wondrous sounds of music
That travel through the air
A flood of auditory waves
In my brain they stick.

Crow

Curious little corvids
Resting on an elevated perch
Overlooking the land
Wonderful, magnificent creatures.

The Life of a Book

Oh, to be a book,
Sitting on a shelf
Your friends at your side
Peace and quiet at last.

With every single checkout,
Begins a new story,
Some good, some bad.

Alas, all things must come to an end,
A rip in a page,
Or a spill on the front,
Ends The Life of a Book.

Summer Shall Hault

Summer..
Season of heat
A time for relaxing
Playing with your friends at the beach
Blissful

Cockatiels

6

Cute little birds
On a eucalyptus branch
Crests of curiosity
Kettle-like whistles
Australian Natives
Today are all over the world
Inquisitive floof
Excellent companions
Love eating their vegetable
Speedy aviators

Maple

Maple leaves fall,
Upon our heads at last
Pumpkin patches,
Halloween
Orange and yellow are the themes
A time for thanks,
And fall parties,
Fallen are those oh so beautiful maple leaves.

Petals

Blooming,
Is a flower
With vibrant petals,
A wondrous feat of nature

Growing,
Is a flower
Tall and strong like a tree
A wondrous feat of nature

Spreading,
Is a flower
Like a wildfire
A wondrous feat of nature

Wilting,
Is a flower
Along it shall pass
A wondrous feat of nature

Sandpiper

Little squeaky bird
Running at the sandy beach
Along they travel

Beach Day

A pebble
Rests in a hot, sandy beach
Wind whistling like a kettle

The ocean
Chilly water on a hot day
Refreshing icon in motion

The seagulls
Squawk and Steal is what they do
Gulls help make your day not dull

Microscopic

Microscopic is our planet
Everyday objects are unseen
Our earth has tiny things in it

A drop of blood is so complex
Many cells of different types
White cells- for invaders they check

Grass

Life is like wild grass-sprouting strong, and
growing tall
Water is needed-for grass to grow tall and strong
Life requires patience-to be healthy and happy
But grass is mowed down-small things can make
you start over

Bells

I hear bells
Bells of holiday
All is calm
Winters here
Snow is falling upon us
Birds are chirping loud

Hen

Hens are loving moms
Caretaker of little chicks
Little Mother bird.

Mom

To my mom,
A wonderful loving human being.
Caring for me at times of sickness and weakness
Always with an open heart.
I cannot express the amount of my love and
gratitude,
For always being by my side.

Dad

To my amazing Dad,
Kind and awesome,
Caring and wholesome.
Thank you so much for always loving me and
taking care of me.
I'm so grateful that you are my dad.
My love and gratitude for you is immeasurable .

Ahma and Nana

To my Ahma and Nana

Ahma, you are so kind and sweet.
Always treating me with delicious food
You help me with anything,
You are so companionate and amazing
I love you so so much.

Nana, you are so sweet and caring.
When I'm sick, you make me hearty meals,
When I'm down, you make me smile,
You are amazing and loved so much.

Ayah and Grandpa

To my Ayah, and my Grandpa

Ayah, you are sweet, amazing and a great
person.
You take me out for golfing,
And always end smiling.
I really appreciate all you do.

Grandpa Roger, you are very kind and loving.
Whenever I talk to you, you are always smiling
and sound happy.
I love you so much.

William

William, you are the best brother anyone could
ask for.
You are so considerate, kind, and compassionate.
Even though we have our times of quarreling,
We resolve together,
And stick together.
You are amazing loving kind, and a great person.
You will succeed greatly in life.

Auntie

Auntie, you are the best!
Every party, and every time we see you
You always have a smile on your face.
I love how you are very outgoing,
You always support me, and help me with rough
times.
Thank you so much for being the loving person
that you are.
I love you so much ch

All Together

The meaning of together,
into companionship or close association.
Dictionary descriptions are accurate to some, but
not others.
To me, together means happiness,
Together means friendship,
Together means love.
Together is not just a word, but a feeling.